Christopher COLUMBUS

Damian Harvey

Illustrated by Mike Phillips

W
FRANKLIN WATTS
LONDON•SYDNEY

Contents

When he was 25, the ship
Columbus was sailing on was
sunk in battle. He held onto an
oar and swam all the way back
to shore.

Columbus went to work in his brother's map shop and spent his time studying. He heard how some people thought the world was flat, like a pancake.

But Columbus knew this wasn't true. He was sure the world was shaped like a pear.

He also knew lots of money could be made by importing fine silk and rare spices from Eastern countries like India and China.

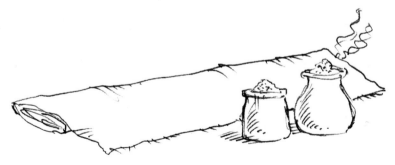

Columbus felt certain it would be quicker to sail West to India. Everyone else sailed East around the bottom of Africa, which was long and dangerous!

"To prove it, I will need lots of money for ships and a crew."

Columbus married a rich Portuguese noblewoman and they had a son called Diego.

Things didn't always go well for Columbus. He went to ask King John II of Portugal for money for his expedition.

"You must be mad," said the King.

Then, not long after Diego was
born, Columbus's wife died.

But he still didn't give
up on his dreams
of discovery…

He told King Ferdinand and Queen Isabella of Spain about his plans. "I will make you rich, and Spain will be even more powerful than before," he promised.

Ferdinand and Isabella were interested in Columbus's idea but they were busy fighting a religious war.

Columbus *still* didn't give up…

"I will bring you gold and jewels, if you make me Admiral of all the Oceans and the Governor of all the New Lands," he declared.

The King and Queen didn't think they would ever see Columbus again, but they eventually agreed to give him money for his voyage to the New World.

CHAPTER 2
Setting Sail

Columbus didn't get as much money as he'd wanted. He only had enough to pay for three small ships.

NINA

PINTA

SANTA MARIA

It wasn't easy finding a crew to sail on this dangerous voyage either. Luckily, his friend Martin Alonso Pinzon knew just where to look.

There were lots of sailors in prison whose only crime was to have a different religion. He set them free.

At 8 o'clock, Columbus set sail in the *Santa Maria* from Palos in Spain.

Martin Alonso followed in the *Pinta*, and his brother, Vincete, was captain of the *Nina*.

Columbus knew it was going to be a difficult journey across the ocean. But he had no idea just how long it was going to take them.

Life on board the ships was hard. Columbus had a cabin but the rest of his crew had to sleep on the deck.

All they had to eat was dried meat and fish, beans and ships biscuit (mixed corn made of barley, rye and bean flour). The crews worked hard to steer the ships and stop them from leaking.

To stop the crews worrying, Columbus pretended they hadn't sailed as far as they really had.

But they sailed for days and the crews became frightened. They thought they would never find land. They even thought they might sail over the edge of the world.

The crews got angry and threatened to throw Columbus overboard. Luckily, Martin Alonso persuaded them not to.

Then someone spotted something in the sea. Columbus knew that land must be near. He told everyone that the first person to spot land would be richly rewarded by the King and Queen.

CHAPTER 3
Land Ahoy!

Then, at 2 o'clock on the 12th October 1492, Rodrigo shouted: "Land ahoy!"

Columbus thought he had discovered a new land to the west of India. He didn't know they were in the Bahamas. It was like discovering a new world.

"I claim this land for the King and Queen of Spain. I name it San Salvador," declared Columbus as he landed.

Columbus was very surprised to find there were people already living on the island.

THEY'VE GOT NO CLOTHES ON!!

The natives were peaceful and friendly. They gave Columbus and his crew lots of exotic gifts, such as beads and parrots.

But Columbus was more interested in their gold. "Where did you get all this yellow stuff?" he wondered.

When it was time to set off again, Martin Alonso sailed one way in search of gold and Columbus went the other way. He explored the islands of Hispaniola, Haiti and Cuba.

CHAPTER 4
Disaster Strikes!

Then, early on Christmas morning… **DISASTER!** The sea was calm and Columbus and his crew were fast asleep. A young boy had been left to steer the ship when…

CRUNCH!!!

The *Santa Maria* ran aground and
fell apart. The crew rescued what
they could and swam ashore.
Their ship was destroyed.

The *Nina* came to the rescue but Columbus had to leave some of his crew behind, as there was no room.

During his journey back to Spain, he thought he saw mermaids swimming in the sea – they weren't as pretty as he'd expected!

The crew that stayed behind made a settlement with the wood that they salvaged from the wrecked ship. They called it 'La Navidad' (Spanish for Christmas).

Crowds of people welcomed Columbus home. The King and Queen were amazed to see him alive. They named Columbus Admiral of the Oceans, just as he had asked.

Then they sent him back to get more gold and to make a Spanish settlement in the New World. This time Columbus took even more ships.

But when Columbus reached the islands, he found the settlement had been destroyed. The crew he'd left behind had been fighting with the natives.

When the new settlers arrived, there was even more fighting.

Many natives grew sick from diseases that had been brought over by the settlers. They had never been in contact with these germs before. New diseases could kill them – even a cold!

Columbus couldn't wait to go and explore south of the islands. But the ships sat for days without any wind.

When they finally reached the island of Trinidad, off the coast of South America, there was only one barrel of water left on board.

Columbus discovered the mouth of the Orinoco River, in Venezuela. With so much fresh water he was sure he had finally found the mainland.

"This could be the Garden of Eden," he thought.

CHAPTER 5
Home in Chains!

But Columbus grew ill and he returned to the Spanish settlement on Hispaniola. When he arrived the settlers were very angry with him.

"Why did we come here?
Where's all the gold and riches
you promised us?" they demanded.

King Ferdinand and Queen Isabella
heard about the trouble in the New
World and they were furious.

"Columbus acts like he is King
of the New World. Arrest him!"

They sent Francisco de Bobadilla, one of their favourite leaders, to investigate what was happening on Hispaniola.

Columbus was arrested and sent back to Spain in chains.

Later, Columbus was given one more chance to find a passage around the world to India.

But this time, there was even more fighting and many ships were sunk by the heavy storms.

Columbus had had enough.

He only set foot in South America, but he is still remembered as the man who discovered America. His voyages changed the world.

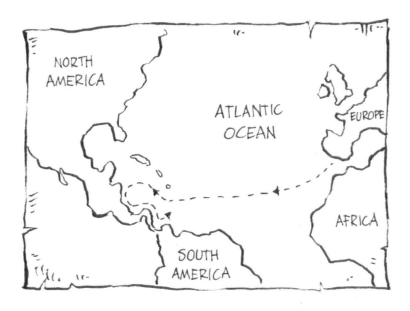

Columbus led the first expedition to the New World and was the first European in the Caribbean and South America. He was a brave explorer and never gave up on his dream of sailing into the unknown.

Timeline

1451   Columbus is born in Genoa.

1476   Columbus's ship is sunk by pirates.

1477   Columbus works in a map shop.

1479   Columbus marries Felipe Perestrello Moniz (daughter of a nobleman).

1480   Columbus's son Diego is born.

1485   Columbus's wife dies.

1486   The King and Queen of Spain refuse to fund Columbus.

1488   Columbus has another son, Fernando. He does not remarry.

1492	King Ferdinand and Queen Isabella of Spain agree to fund Columbus.
1492	3rd August: Columbus sets sail from Palos, Spain on the *Santa Maria*.
	12th October: Columbus lands in the Bahamas and claims the land for Spain. He names it San Salvador.
	25th December: the *Santa Maria* runs aground and sinks. His crew create a settlement called 'La Navidad'.
1493	March: Columbus returns to Palos, Spain and tells of his discoveries.
	September: Columbus explores Hispaniola and established a settlement in Haiti.

1494	Columbus returns to Spain.
1498	Columbus makes his third voyage. He lands at the Cape Verde islands. He is the first Euopean to land there and to find pearls.
1500	Francisco de Bobadilla is orderd to arrest Columbus and bring him back to Spain as a prisoner.
1502	Columbus is freed and makes his fourth and final voyage.
1504	Columbus returns to Spain.
1506	20th May: Columbus dies in Valladolid, Spain.

First published in 2014 by
Franklin Watts
338 Euston Road
London NW1 3BH

Franklin Watts Australia
Level 17/207 Kent Street
Sydney NSW 2000

HB ISBN 978 1 4451 3293 8
PB ISBN 978 14451 3294 5
Library ebook ISBN 978 1 4451 3296 9
ebook ISBN 978 1 4451 3295 2

Dewey Decimal Classification Number: 920

Series editor: Melanie Palmer
Series designer Cathryn Gilbert

Printed in Great Britain

Franklin Watts is a division of Hachette Children's Books,
an Hachette UK company.
www.hachette.co.uk